Arthur Daou

Edward FitzGerald's

Rubaiyat of Omar Khayyam

First Edition

In Colloquial Lebanese Arabic

First published in the United States in 2009 by Antony Daou, under the **BlackCat Imprint**, a division of

Black Cat Ventures, 195 Main Street, Sharon Springs, NY 13459

ISBN No. 978-0-9825666-1-9

To my wife,

Nana

Edward FitzGerald

On the occasion of the 150th anniversary of

Edward FitzGerald's First Edition, 1859

& the 50th anniversary of
Arthur Daou's
first translation, 1959

Omar Khayyam, astronomer, mathematician, poet, lived in Naishapur the capital of Khorassan. He died in the early part of the Twelfth Century AD, leaving behind, among a vast body of work, a collection of quatrains, a hand-written manuscript of which made its way to the Bodleian Library at Oxford. From this copy, the English poet Edward FitzGerald, in 1859, published his first translation comprising 75 quatrains.

These quatrains of FitzGerald are not translations but really new poetry. For in these archaic stanzas FitzGerald found the true arrow to fit the bow of his extraordinary poetic gift.

This is certainly not the first Arabic translation of Omar Khayyam's Rubaiyat. Several famous translations from the Persian precede it, including versions by some of the greatest Arab poets: Ahmad el-Safi al-Najafi, Ahmad Rami, Wadih al-Boustani and Jamil al-Mala'ika.

The significance of this work by Arthur Daou is that it is the first translation of FitzGerald into Arabic, *and* that it is in colloquial (Lebanese) Arabic. Daou took FitzGerald's approach to create a new poem, faithful to the original, yet true to the voice of Khayyam. In Daou's case, he used FitzGerald's stanzas as the structural basis for his quatrains.

Arthur was championed by Yusuf al-Khal, the prominent Arab poet and publisher, and *Dar Majalat al-Shi'ir* issued a first edition in 1962. That first edition is long since out of print. This new edition, ten years after Arthur's death in 1999 is an interesting and important addition that should stand out even among the many editions of the Rubaiyat.

Many years later, Arthur achieved prominence as a naturalist and a champion of Lebanon's remarkable yet sadly neglected natural resources. Farid Salman, the Lebanese poet and head of the Kahlil Gibran Society, eulogized him as a "Prophet of the Earth."

Edward FitzGerald's First Edition of The

Rubaiyat

Of Omar Khayyam

1

Awake! for Morning in the Bowl of Night
Has flung the Stone that puts the Stars to Flight:
And Lo! the Hunter of the East has caught
The Sultan's Turret in a Noose of Light.

2

Dreaming when Dawn's Left Hand was in the Sky
I heard a Voice within the Tavern cry,
"Awake, my Little Ones, and fill the Cup
Before Life's Liquor in its Cup be dry."

3

And, as the Cock crew, those who stood before
The Tavern shouted—"Open then the Door.
You know how little while we have to stay,
And, once departed, may return no more."

4

Now the New Year reviving old Desires,
The thoughtful Soul to Solitude retires,
Where the White Hand of Moses on the Bough
Puts out, and Jesus from the Ground suspires.

5

Iram indeed is gone with all its Rose,
And Jamshyd's Sev'n-ring'd Cup where no one knows;
But still the Vine her ancient Ruby yields,
And still a Garden by the Water blows.

6

And David's Lips are lock't; but in divine
High piping Pelevi, with "Wine! Wine! Wine!
Red Wine!"—the Nightingale cries to the Rose
That yellow Cheek of hers to incarnadine.

7

Come, fill the Cup, and in the Fire of Spring
The Winter Garment of Repentance fling:
The Bird of Time has but a little way
To fly—and Lo! the Bird is on the Wing.

8

And look—a thousand Blossoms with the Day
Woke—and a thousand scatter'd into Clay:
And this first Summer Month that brings the Rose
Shall take Jamshyd and Kaikobad away.

9

But come with old Khayyam, and leave the Lot
Of Kaikobad and Kaikhosru forgot:
Let Rustum lay about him as he will,
Or Hatim Tai cry Supper—heed them not.

10

With me along some Strip of Herbage strown
That just divides the desert from the sown,
Where name of Slave and Sultan scarce is known,
And pity Sultan Mahmud on his Throne.

11

Here with a Loaf of Bread beneath the Bough,
A Flask of Wine, a Book of Verse—and Thou
Beside me singing in the Wilderness—
And Wilderness is Paradise enow.

12

"How sweet is mortal Sovranty!"—think some:
Others—"How blest the Paradise to come!"
Ah, take the Cash in hand and waive the Rest;
Oh, the brave Music of a distant Drum!

13

Look to the Rose that blows about us—"Lo,
Laughing," she says, "into the World I blow:
At once the silken Tassel of my Purse
Tear, and its Treasure on the Garden throw."

14

The Worldly Hope men set their Hearts upon
Turns Ashes—or it prospers; and anon,
Like Snow upon the Desert's dusty Face
Lighting a little Hour or two—is gone.

15

And those who husbanded the Golden Grain,
And those who flung it to the Winds like Rain,
Alike to no such aureate Earth are turn'd
As, buried once, Men want dug up again.

16

Think, in this batter'd Caravanserai
Whose Doorways are alternate Night and Day,
How Sultan after Sultan with his Pomp
Abode his Hour or two, and went his way.

17

They say the Lion and the Lizard keep
The Courts where Jamshyd gloried and drank deep:
And Bahram, that great Hunter—the Wild Ass
Stamps o'er his Head, and he lies fast asleep.

18

I sometimes think that never blows so red
The Rose as where some buried Caesar bled;
That every Hyacinth the Garden wears
Dropt in its Lap from some once lovely Head.

19

And this delightful Herb whose tender Green
Fledges the River's Lip on which we lean—
Ah, lean upon it lightly! for who knows
From what once lovely Lip it springs unseen!

20

Ah! my Beloved, fill the Cup that clears
TO-DAY of past Regrets and future Fears-
To-morrow?—Why, To-morrow I may be
Myself with Yesterday's Sev'n Thousand Years.

21

Lo! some we loved, the loveliest and the best
That Time and Fate of all their Vintage prest,
Have drunk their Cup a Round or two before,
And one by one crept silently to Rest.

22

And we, that now make merry in the Room
They left, and Summer dresses in new Bloom,
Ourselves must we beneath the Couch of Earth
Descend, ourselves to make a Couch—
for whom?

23

Ah, make the most of what we yet may spend,
Before we too into the Dust Descend;
Dust into Dust, and under Dust, to lie,
Sans Wine, sans Song, sans Singer and –
sans End!

24

Alike for those who for TO-DAY prepare,
And those that after a TO-MORROW stare,
A Muezzin from the Tower of Darkness cries
"Fools! your Reward is neither Here nor There."

25

Why, all the Saints and Sages who discuss'd
Of the Two Worlds so learnedly, are thrust
Like foolish Prophets forth; their Words to Scorn
Are scatter'd, and their Mouths are stopt with Dust.

26

Oh, come with old Khayyam, and leave the Wise
To talk; one thing is certain, that Life flies;
One thing is certain, and the Rest is Lies;
The Flower that once has blown for ever dies.

27

Myself when young did eagerly frequent
Doctor and Saint, and heard great Argument
About it and about: but evermore
Came out by the same Door as in I went.

28

With them the Seed of Wisdom did I sow,
And with my own hand labour'd it to grow:
And this was all the Harvest that I reap'd—
"I came like Water, and like Wind I go."

29

Into this Universe, and why not knowing,
Nor whence, like Water willy-nilly flowing:
And out of it, as Wind along the Waste,
I know not whither, willy-nilly blowing.

30

What, without asking, hither hurried whence?
And, without asking, whither hurried hence!
Another and another Cup to drown
The Memory of this Impertinence!

31

Up from Earth's Centre through the seventh Gate
I rose, and on the Throne of Saturn sate,
And many Knots unravel'd by the Road;
But not the Knot of Human Death and Fate.

32

There was a Door to which I found no Key:
There was a Veil past which I could not see:
Some little Talk awhile of ME and THEE
There seemed—and then no more of THEE and ME.

33

Then to the rolling Heav'n itself I cried,
Asking, "What Lamp had Destiny to guide
Her little Children stumbling in the Dark?"
And—"A blind understanding!" Heav'n replied.

34

Then to this earthen Bowl did I adjourn
My Lip the secret Well of Life to learn:
And Lip to Lip it murmur'd—"While you live,
Drink!—for once dead you never shall return."

35

I think the Vessel, that with fugitive
Articulation answer'd, once did live,
And merry-make; and the cold Lip I kiss'd
How many Kisses might it take—and give.

36

For in the Market-place, one Dusk of Day,
I watch'd the Potter thumping his wet Clay:
And with its all obliterated Tongue
It murmur'd—"Gently, Brother, gently, pray!"

37

Ah, fill the Cup:—what boots it to repeat
How Time is slipping underneath our Feet:
Unborn TO-MORROW and dead YESTERDAY,
Why fret about them if TO-DAY be sweet!

38

One Moment in Annihilation's Waste,
One moment, of the Well of Life to taste—
The Stars are setting, and the Caravan
Starts for the dawn of Nothing—Oh, make haste!

39

How long, how long, in infinite Pursuit
Of This and That endeavour and dispute?
Better be merry with the fruitful Grape
Than sadden after none, or bitter, Fruit.

40

You know, my Friends, how long since in my House
For a new Marriage I did make Carouse:
Divorced old barren Reason from my Bed,
And took the Daughter of the Vine to Spouse.

41

For "IS" and "IS-NOT" though with Rule and Line,
And, "UP-AND-DOWN" without, I could define,
I yet in all I only cared to know,
Was never deep in anything but—Wine.

42

And lately, by the Tavern Door agape,
Came stealing through the Dusk an Angel Shape,
Bearing a vessel on his Shoulder; and
He bid me taste of it; and 'twas—the Grape!

43

The Grape that can with Logic absolute
The Two-and-Seventy jarring Sects confute:
The subtle Alchemist that in a Trice
Life's leaden Metal into Gold transmute.

44

The mighty Mahmud, the victorious Lord,
That all the misbelieving and black Horde
Of Fears and Sorrows that infest the Soul
Scatters and slays with his enchanted Sword.

45

But leave the Wise to wrangle, and with me
The Quarrel of the Universe let be:
And, in some corner of the Hubbub coucht,
Make Game of that which makes as much of Thee.

46

For in and out, above, about, below,
'Tis nothing but a Magic Shadow-show,
Play'd in a Box whose Candle is the Sun,
Round which we Phantom Figures come and go.

47

And if the Wine you drink, the Lip you press,
End in the Nothing all Things end in—Yes-
Then fancy while Thou art, Thou art but what
Thou shalt be—Nothing—Thou shalt not be less.

48

While the Rose blows along the River Brink,
With old Khayyam the Ruby Vintage drink:
And when the Angel with his darker Draught
Draws up to thee—take that, and do not shrink.

49

'Tis all a Chequer-board of Nights and Days
Where Destiny with Men for Pieces plays:
Hither and thither moves, and mates, and slays,
And one by one back in the Closet lays.

50

The Ball no Question makes of Ayes and Noes,
But Right or Left as strikes the Player goes;
And He that toss'd Thee down into the Field,
He knows about it all—HE knows—HE knows!

51

The Moving Finger writes; and, having writ,
Moves on: nor all thy Piety nor Wit
Shall lure it back to cancel half a Line,
Nor all thy Tears wash out a Word of it.

52

And that inverted Bowl we call The Sky,
Whereunder crawling coop't we live and die,
Lift not thy hands to IT for help—for It
Rolls impotently on as Thou or I.

53

With Earth's first Clay They did the Last Man's knead,
And then of the Last Harvest sow'd the Seed:
Yea, the first Morning of Creation wrote
What the Last Dawn of Reckoning shall read.

54

I tell Thee this—When, starting from the Goal,
Over the shoulders of the flaming Foal
Of Heav'n Parwin and Mushtari they flung,
In my predestin'd Plot of Dust and Soul

55

The Vine had struck a Fibre; which about
It clings my Being—let the Sufi flout;
Of my Base Metal may be filed a Key,
That shall unlock the Door he howls without.

56

And this I know: whether the one True Light,
Kindle to Love, or Wrath consume me quite,
One Glimpse of It within the Tavern caught
Better than in the Temple lost outright.

57

Oh Thou who didst with Pitfall and with Gin
Beset the Road I was to wander in,
Thou wilt not with Predestination round
Enmesh me, and impute my Fall to Sin?

58

Oh Thou, who Man of baser Earth didst make,
And who with Eden didst devise the Snake;
For all the Sin wherewith the Face of Man
Is blacken'd, Man's Forgiveness give—and take!

Derek Jensen (Tysto), 2005-September-03

Kuza – Nama

The Book of Pots

59

Listen again. One Evening at the Close
Of Ramazan, ere the better Moon arose,
In that old Potter's Shop I stood alone
With the clay Population round in Rows.

60

And strange to tell, among that Earthen Lot
Some could articulate, while others not:
And suddenly one more impatient cried—
"Who is the Potter, pray, and who the Pot?"

61

Then said another — "Surely not in vain
My substance from the common Earth was ta'en,
That He who subtly wrought me into Shape
Should stamp me back to common Earth again."

62

Another said — "Why, ne'er a peevish Boy
Would break the Bowl from which he drank in Joy;
Shall He that made the Vessel in pure Love
And Fancy, in an after Rage destroy!"

63

None answer'd this; but after Silence spake
A Vessel of a more ungainly Make:
"They sneer at me for leaning all awry;
What? did the Hand then of the Potter shake?"

64

Said one — "Folks of a surly Tapster tell,
And daub his Visage with the Smoke of Hell;
They talk of some strict Testing of us — Pish!
He's a Good Fellow, and 'twill all be well."

65

Then said another with a long-drawn Sigh,
"My Clay with long oblivion is gone dry:
But, fill me with the old familiar Juice,
Methinks I might recover by-and-bye!"

66

So, while the Vessels one by one were speaking,
One spied the little Crescent all were seeking:
And then they jogg'd each other, "Brother! Brother!
Hark to the Porter's Shoulder-knot a-creaking!"

67

Ah, with the Grape my fading Life provide,
And wash my Body whence the life has died,
And in a Windingsheet of Vineleaf wrapt,
So bury me by some sweet Garden-side.

68

That ev'n my buried Ashes such a Snare
Of Perfume shall fling up into the Air,
As not a True Believer passing by
But shall be overtaken unaware.

69

Indeed, the Idols I have loved so long
Have done my Credit in Men's Eye much wrong:
Have drown'd my Honour in a shallow Cup,
And sold my Reputation for a Song.

70

Indeed, indeed, Repentance oft before
I swore—but was I sober when I swore?
And then and then came Spring, and Rose-in-hand
My thread-bare Penitence a-pieces tore.

71

And much as Wine has play'd the Infidel,
And robb'd me of my Robe of Honour—well,
I often wonder what the Vintners buy
One half so precious as the Goods they sell?

72

Alas, that Spring should vanish with the Rose!
That Youth's sweet-scented Manuscript should close!
The Nightingale that in the Branches sang,
Ah, whence, and whither flown again,
who knows!

73

Ah, Love! could thou and I with Fate conspire
To grasp this sorry Scheme of Things entire,
Would not we shatter it to bits—and then
Re-mould it nearer to the Heart's Desire!

74

Ah, Moon of my Delight who know'st no wane,
The Moon of Heav'n is rising once again:
How oft hereafter rising shall she look
Through this same Garden after me—in vain!

75

And when Thyself with shining Foot shall pass
Among the Guests Star-scatter'd on The Grass,
And in Thy joyous Errand reach the Spot
Where I made one—turn down an empty Glass!

Tamam Shud

تمام شد

٧٤

يا قمر افراح قلبي اللي اكتمل ،
بدر السما شي طل من فوق الجبل :
ياما وياما بعـــد عَ دربه يعود
يسأل عليّي وكل مرّه بلا امل !

٧٥

ولمّن يا ساقي متل ميي بساقيه
تروي الضيوف لْعل عشب متراميه ،
وبدورتك هالمفرحه توصل مكان ،
مطرح مكاني ، طب كاسه فاضيه .

٧٢

ويلي الربيع يزول وتزول الورود !
وتعود صفحات الصبا لطيّ الوجود !
هاك الكنار العن يغرد عالغصون ،
من وين جا ولوين مِنْ يدري يعود !

٧٣

يا حب لو بمقامره مع هالقدر
فينا قبضنا هالدني الكلاّ كدر ،
قولك مَ كنَا لألفْ نتفه منسحقا
ومنعيد صبّا عَ هوى قلب و نظر !

٧٠

ويامـا ويامـا حلفت ، من قبل ، الندم ـ
بس قولك كنت صاحي بهالقسم ؟
وعاد الربيع بموكبه الزاهي اجا
وكل اللي بنيت توبتي عليها هدم .

٧١

ومهما الخمر بمظهر الكافر ظهر ،
ومزّق لباس معزّتي بين البشر ـ
محتار هالخمّار شو عم يشْتري
هل قيمته بشي نص يل باعه اختمر !

٦٨

حتى ترابي اللي انطوى يبقى يبوح
مع كل هبّة ، عطر ، بالنسمه يفوح ،
تَى ولا صِديّق ان مرّ الطريق
الا وقلبه ، بلا وعي ، بصدره يلوح .

٦٩

مؤكد الاصنام لْعبدتا طويل
هالعمر عند الناس تركتني ذليل :
غرقّت فخري بكاسه فايشه
وباعت مقامي باقلّ من القليل .

٦٧

داوو بدوى العنقود هالعمر القصير ،

ومن بعد موتي غسّلو جسمي بعصير ،

وبوراق كرمه لفلفوني ، واجعلو

قبري بحديقه قربها العابر يسير .

٦٥

وعاد واحد قال وبلهجة اسف ،
من طول هالنسيان فخاري نشف :
« بس لولا بنتلي بهاك العصير
بظني عمهل بردّ يلْ قلبي نزف . »

٦٦

وما بين ما الفخار عن يحكو ، قشع
واحد مبينن هل هلال الْشي طلع ؛
وراحو يهزّو كل واحد صاحبه
من جهّة العصّار للهزّ استمع . »

٦٣

هيدا بقي بلا جواب ؛ والعاد وحكي
واحد قبيح الشكل عَ جنبه تكي :
« بيعروني بجلستي وشكلي القبيح
« شو ، كانت الفنان ايده ملبّكي؟ »

٦٤

قال واحد ، « قوم عن ساقي لئيم
حكيو ، ولقيو بعتبته غبار الجحيم ؛
بيحدثو عن تجربه شديده وحساب
كيف ، شب مليح ، والآتي نعيم ! »

٦١

« مؤكد » ، الثاني قال ، « في قصد ونوى
تَى منِ التراب انشال هلّ صُلبي احتوى ،
يبقى العطاني شكل من فنّه يعيـــد
للـتراب تراب في ضلعي انطوى . »

٦٢

واحتار غيره ـ « ولا صبي منكِ رغب
حتى يكسّر كاس طابت بالشرب ؛
وكيف البدع هالكاس من وحي وخيال ،
رح يكسره من بعد شي ثورة غضب ! »

٥٩

واسماع ، ليله بآخرة شهر الصيام ،
وشي قبل ما لهلال بيّنله قوام ،
ما بين قوم الطين لحالي بقيت
وصفوف هالبرقان من خلف وامام

٦٠

والعجب ، ما بين هرجن والزعيق
تمكنت افهم قول هونيكِ فريق ؛
والا وينن صاح واحد « دخلكن
شو الفرق بين الكوّنه وبين البريق ؟ »

Photo taken by Randy Oostdyk, and released under GFDL.

كتاب الفخّار

٥٧

يا من رسمت الدرب يلْ فيهـا نسير ،
وجعلت فيها التجربه وبنت العصير ،
كيف بـدّك تحسب علي زنوب
واللي ارتكبته تقرر بخط المصير ؟

٥٨

يـلْ من ضعيف الطين كونت البشر ،
ول مع الجنّه نهيت ثمره من الثمر ؛
رغم الخطـايا كلهـا السوّد بهـــا
الانسان وجهُه غفر ، حتى للكفر .

٥٥

العنقـــود حرك بين اعوادي وتر
خلّي الصوفي يلوم ، لو صبحّ وطر :
ممكن المفتاح هل من معـــدني
ينصاغ ، يفتح باب برّاته نطرْ .

٥٦

ولو النـــور الحق للحب انضرم ،
او للغضب وبلهبته يبقى عدم :
بفضّل بحانه مش بمعبد المحو :
ولنّه اندمت يكون لُه نفع الندم .

٥٣

جبلو باوّل طين آخر مِنْ رضع ،
ومِنْ حَب آخر موسم بداره انزرع :
ايه ، واول يوم بالعـــالم كتب
يلْ رح بتقرا الآخره ورح ينسمع .

٥٤

وهالقد بقدر قول لمّا مْنِ الاخير
بديو ، مفوق الشمس شعلة هالاثير ،
نثرو الثريا ، المشترى ، وباقي النجوم
بين اللي هوّه لْطينطي صبّح مصير .

٥١

الاصبع اللي خَطْ والدايم يخط
ما فيك قوه تجبره يكتب غلط :
لا الدمع يحزف حرف من بين الحروف ،
ولا الحلم يقدر يقنعه يغيّر نقط .

٥٢

وهالطاسة البلقلب هالإسما السما ،
ولتحتها ، تيموت ، هالقلب ارتما ،
صوبا ، لا ترفع ديك ، حتى تساعدك ،
متاك ومتلي دايرا وقيدا العما .

٤٩

هالكون «داما» محزّمي بليل ونهار
فوقا القدر والناس ما بينن حجار:
هوني لهوني ينقلو، يردّو، يجو،
وقطعه وقطعه يْريجعو لخلف الستار.

٥٠

الطابه منين لوين ما بتعمل طلب،
ولكن بتوقع كيف ما اللاعب ضرب؛
وهوّه الطرحنا فوق هالملعب، إله
علم السبب، له علم عن اصل السبب

٤٧

وان كان كاس التشرب وخصر التضم ،

متل غيرن للعدم يبقو ـ نعم ـ

تصوّر مدامك بعد ـ منّك هالعدم

يلْ رح تصير ـ ومش اقلّ مُن العدم .

٤٨

وما دام هالورده على الضفه تميل ،

اشرب مع الخيام هالخمر العليل

ولمّا الملاك يقدم بكاسه إلك

خلّه الكريه ـ شراب لا تولّي ذليل .

٤٥

خلّي الحكيم يبقبش سرار القـــدر
وانسى صراع الكون ، متلي ، والعبر ،
وبي زاويـه من هالخليطـه القايمه
تلاعب عللي فيك هالقد افتكر .

٤٦

وْلأنـ فوق وتحت وبعيد وقريب ،
اشباح فرجة سحرَ عَ مسرح عجيب ،
جوات علبـه الشمس تلعب شمعتـا ،
ونحنا قبـالا طيوف منطلّ ونغيب .

٤٣

العنقـود يللي بيقـدر بفعل وسبب
يصلح بمنطق خلفـة صحاب الشعب :
عالم كماوي بيقدر بلحظه يـدير
نحس الدني ونحاسهـا سبايك دهب .

٤٤

بي قدرتُه ، محمـود هالمولى العنيـد ،
يلْ كل اهل الزندقـه وجيش العبيـد
من خوف من احزان هالتبـلي النفوس
بسيفه العجيب يْبـدد صفوفا ويبيـد .

٤١

الاسباب ، اني بدرك قْريب وبعيد ،
وبقدر بحلّل معدن رصاص وحديد ،
لكن بكل الردت اني افهمه ،
ما قدرت غوص كتير الا بالنبيـد .

٤٢

ومش من زمان ْبباب هالخان انسحب ،
بين الدغوش ، ْملاك ولحدّي اقترب
حامــــل عكتفه بريق عللني تدوق ؛
وكان السقاني عصير عنقود العنب !

٣٩

وْلأي حدّ وآخره بجدّ وجدل
بلا آخره للكد ، اتعاب العمل ؟
الفين احلى تسعد ببنت الكروم
من شي تمر بالمرّ والقهر انحصل

٤٠

وبتعرفو يا صحاب عمرا لفرحتي
يومْ اللي عرس جديد دشّن عتبتي :
طلقت بنت المنطق الجردا العجوز ،
وعطيت بنت الخمر نص مخدتي .

٣٧

يلا نعبي الـكاس شو بينفع نقول
كيف الزمن من بين ايدينـا يزول :
مبارح اللي مات ، بكرا الما ولد
شو نفعهن واليـوم لللذه وصول .

٣٨

نتفة زمن ما بين كومات الفنا ،
نتفة بنبع العمر متحلل لنـــا ـ
النجم عم بيشح ، واليطفي النجوم ـ
يللا نعجل ـــ صار ظلّه ببابنا !

٣٥

بظني الكاس ، الْتمتم بهاك الكلام ،
كان بالزمان يعيش ويعاطي المدام ؛
وهالشفّة ال قبلتهـــا الملهـا حيـاة
كم قبله بتاخد وتعطي تمام !

٣٦

لش بذكر تفرجت مرّه بالطريق
عَ شخص عمن يجبـل بطينه بريق :
ولسان هاك الطين يلْ باقي يقول ـــ
« دخلك يا خي كون بحْوالي رفيق . »

٣٣

وعنـدا سألت الفيك ــ في هل ورا
ستـار العوالم يشتغـــل يا هل ترا
يوجد علامه تقودني في هالطريق ؟
جاب اللي في « فهم اعمى شو درى . »

٣٤

وبعدا لشفة كاس من جبـــلة تراب
ملتلا ولقيت عَ شْفافا الجواب :
قالت ما عشت شراب مش ممكن تعود
لهالدني والموت صاير عَ البواب .

٣١

عْليت سابع باب في عـــالي الأثير
وْجلست عَ عرش الزحل ، فوق السرير ،
وياما عقَـد حلّيت في دربي وعصت
هاك اللي هوّه شدها بسرّ المصير.

٣٢

لقيت باب وبس ما قدرت الدخـول ،
وحجاب خلفُه تحرّم لْعيني الوصول :
عني وعنك قول في برهـــه انحكى ،
برهه ، وبعـدا بطّل القايـل يقول.

٢٩

لها لدني ، وليش جيت نفسي ما دِرِتْ ،
ولا منين ، متـل المي عالخيره جِرِت
وبعدين ، متل الريح بصحاري الفلا ،
لوين ما لي علم ، عالخـــيره سِرِت .

٣٠

شو ، بدون سئـال ، لهوني منين ؟
وبدون ايّا سئـال ، من هوني لوين !
الف كاس بـكاس بـــدّا المسأله
بلـكي الاهـاني بتنتسا ولنّه لحين .

٢٧

ذاتي برغبه لْفِيْتْ في عهد الشباب
عَ عالم وقدّيس ، ولجدل وخطاب
تسمعت ، لكن كل مرّه زرتهن ـــ
مطرح ما فت طلعت من ذات البواب .

٢٨

بلهفه ، بذور المعرفه زرعنا سوا
وعنتا بذاتي لحد ما حبًّا استوى :
وكل يلّلي جنيت من هاك الحصاد ـــ
جيت متل المي ، بِرْحَل كالهوا .

٢٥

وهودي بتقوى وعلم يلْ طلبو جواب
عن هالدني وهيديك والحكيو بصواب
صبّح مصيرن متل اهل الزندقه
قولن طعـــام الريح وبتمّن تراب .

٢٦

اشرب معي واتروك شو يْقول الخبير
من دون شك العمر في سرعه يطير ؛
من دون ايا شك والباقي حكي —
الورده الصّار وفتحت موتا المصير .

٢٣

دونك نقضّي كل يلْ باقي لنـا
من قبل ما الايام تطوي شملنـا ؛
غبره لغبره وتحت غبره ننطوي
بلا آخره ، بلا خمر ، ومغنّي وغنا .

٢٤

عالسوا لْهلّي بيبنو لْهَنْهَار ،
واللي بيكـره بيحلمو بأجر ومزار ،
اذّن عليهن صوت من برج الظـلام
« مجانين ! ما في أجر في أيَّا ديار . »

٢١

وليك اللي كنا نحب هل احلا واغرّ
شو الدهر عالايام من كرمه عصر ،
شربو خمورن كم دورا قبلنا
وعالسكت راحو وما رجع منهن خبر

٢٢

ونحنا اللي هلق مطرح التركو نعين
موكب لصيف جديد ونراعي الحنين ،
لا بد متلن تحت فرشه من تراب
ننزل ، ونحنا نفرش الفرشه لمين ؟

١٩

وهالعشْاب المفرحه العرقا تكي
عَ جنب شفة نهر فوقا نتكي ـ
استلقي عليها بلطف يمكن تربتا
شفه جميله غاب عن تما الحكي .

٢٠

عبّي حبيبي كاس يجلي هالمسا
من هم بكرا ومن اسف امس واسا ـ
الغد ؟ ليش الغد ؟ يمكن إنْوجد
مع الف سبع سنين من امس انتسا .

١٧

بيخبروني السبع والحردون سكن
ديوان فيها جمشد تغنّى ومَجَنْ ،
وبهرام ، ربّ الصيد ، غافي ما يفيق
بتمرّ فوقه العير ما بيحرك بدن .

١٨

لي ظن ما في ورد لُه حمره عَ قدْ
هل طل مطرح دمّ شي قيصر جمد ؛
ويا بكل فلّه هالجنينه تزيّنت
وقعت بحضنا من حلو بماضي الامد

١٥

وهالجمّعو الحبات يلْ لونا ذهب ،
والبدروها بالهوى من غير سبب ،
تنينْ مصارو ، بعدما انطمرو ، تراب
أصفر تعاد العاش عن تربْ نقب .

١٦

تأملو ، بهالخان يلْ عليو الغبار
واللي بوابه مداوره ليل ونهار ،
كم في سلطان قضّو ساعتن
فيها وراحو خلف هديك الديار .

١٣

ليكو الوردي تقول مع مَيْل الهوى ـ
« بلاقي الدني عن بيتسم كلي سوا
بفتّح ، وبفْتح صِرّتي القِبْعَا حرير
وعَ الحْنينه بْزِتّ شو كنزي احتوى . »

١٤

بهالدني الآمال يلْ حلما البشر
يمّا بتبقى رماد يبتعطي ثمر ،
حالن ومدري تلج عَ صحرا سقط
برهـه ، وبعدا ما بقي منّه اثر

١١

هون فيّة غصن ومحزّز نبيد
ورغيف خبز ودفتر وريشه وقصيد
وانت حدّي عم تغنّي بهالفلا
الفردوس هوني قدْ ما قلبي يْريد.

١٢

البعض همن عزّ هوني بهالدني
والبعض بالفردوس حلمن منبني؛
قْباض اللي هلّق يْنصرف وانسى الوعود
وانسى الطبول المن بعيد مأذّنِه!

٩

تركهن يْروحو ، ليش نشغـــل بالنـا
بجمشد ، بكيكوباد ، شو نفعن لنا ؛
خلّي لحـاتم طي آيات الكـرم
ورستم وبيّه بالوغى يهزّو القنـــا .

١٠

وْتعـا معي لَ مرج بالعشب امتلا ،
شي يْحد بين الزرع وْصحاري الفلا ،
مطرح بْلا سلطان وجْنود وعبيـــد
وفي عطف عَ محمود يلْ عرش اعتلا .

٧

عبّي الكاس ْوزتْ في نار الربيع
توب الندم يلْ لَبسك عهد الصقيع ؛
طير الزمن يا صاح مشواره قصير ـــ
وهالطير ، متل الطير ، قديشه سريع .

٨

شي ألف ورده كل صبح بيطلعو
وشي ألف غيرن للتراب ْبيرجعو ؛
وهالشهر يلّلي جاب وردات الربيع
جمشد وكيكوباد رح ياخد معهُ .

٥

إيرام راحت ما بقي منها اثر ،
وجمشد وكاسو ، وين ما عنا خبر ؛
وبعدو عَ عهدو الكرم بِخمرُهْ كريم ،
وباقي جناين وردها بيروي النظر .

٦

وداوود ريقُهْ جفّ ؛ لكن هالكنار ،
بصوتُهْ الجميل ولغتُهْ الملها غيار ،
يْنادي « نبيد ! نبيد ! » للوردهِ و« نبيد ــ
احمر » يْرِدّ اللون لخدودا القمار .

٣

وِلِمْ صاح الديك ، والبرّا صحو ،
نادو « فتاح الباب ، عجّلْ وافتحو !
حان الرحيل ووقتنا الباقي قليـــل
هيهات نرجع بعد حانك نلمحو . »

٤

العـــام الجديد بْطلْتو يهيّج ولوع ،
للتـــأمُّل مالت الروح بْرجوع ،
مطرح مَ موسى بايد بيضا عالغصون
مد بعطى ، وبالارض يتنهّد يسوع .

١

فيقو ، جيوش الشمس في ساح النزال
هزمو جيوش الليل واحتلّو الجبال
قلبو العتم لَ فيّ بي وادي ووطى
ومدّو لبرج القصر بالمرجه خيـال.

٢

حالم ، وخيط الفجر شي انّه ابتــدا
بذكر كأني سمعت بالحانـه نـدا ،
« فيقو يا ولْدي وامرحو واملو الكؤوس
من قبــل ما الأيام ينشف موردا . »

ليست هذه الرباعيات لفتزجرالد موضوع ترجمة و حسب، بل لقد وجد فيها السهم المنشود لقوس شاعريته الجبار. ذلك أن ترجمة فتزجرالد للرباعيات تعد من أجمل ما نظم في الشعر الانكليزي.

و هذه الترجمة العربية لرباعيات عمر الخيام، كما نقلها فيتزجرالد إلى اللغة الانكليزية، ليست الاولى ؛ إذ قد سبقها ترجمات عديدة منها لاحمد الصافي النجفي، و أحمد رامي، و وديع البستاني، و جميل الملائكة. و لكن المهم في هذه الترجمة لارثر ضو، هو أنها باللغة العربية (أو اللبنانية) الدارجة. ترجمها أرثر عام ١٩٥٩ و نشرها يوسف الخال لاول مرة عام ١٩٦٢ في دار مجلة الشعر.

عمر الخيام شاعر فارسي عاش في نيشابور، عاصمة خراسان، و توفي في أوائل القرن الثاني عشر، تاركاً، فيما ترك، مجموعة قصائد عثر على نسخة خطية لها في مكتبة بوديليان باكسفورد.

و عن هذه النسخة، أخرج الشاعر الانكليزي ادورد فتزجرالد عام ١٨٥٩، أول ترجمة للرباعيات حوت ٧٥ رباعية.

8 25 '95

إلى

زوجتي

نانا

Black Cat Ventures,
Sharon Springs, NY 13459

ISBN No. 978-0-9825666-1-9

ارثر ضو

رباعيات

عمر الخيام

في اللغة اللبنانية الدارجة

www.ingramcontent.com/pod-product-compliance
Lightning Source LLC
LaVergne TN
LVHW010115170826
845678LV00012B/2416
9780982566619